Printed in Great Britain
by Amazon

35685044R00071